How Did Things Get So Off Course

How Did Things Get So Off Course

Juanita Kuwik

ARCHWAY
PUBLISHING

Archway Publishing books may be ordered through booksellers or by contacting:

Archway Publishing
1663 Liberty Drive
Bloomington, IN 47403
www.archwaypublishing.com
844-669-3957

ISBN: 978-1-6657-6763-7 (sc)
ISBN: 978-1-6657-6764-4 (e)

Library of Congress Control Number: 2024922529

Print information available on the last page.

Archway Publishing rev. date: 11/13/2024

Contents

Contents

Introduction

"How did things get so off course" is an anthology of poems put together for a journey.

A journey through love, life, family & politics during an era of chaos, confusion, and uncertainty. Just as these three feelings are apart of many of our lives; so is love, compassion, and a good sense of humor!

As an adult reader you can expect to experience a wide range of emotions while reading this book. This book may not be suitable for young readers. It is my intent to relay thoughts and experiences that may affect us all at some time in our lives, be it funny or sad. When you read this book, it is my sincere hope that you can relate to many of the poems, allowing you to reflect on your own experiences in life, good and bad.

I like to travel and have had the good fortune to be able to do so. Most of my travels have been around the United States, but as a child I spent time in Japan. I have also spent time in Mexico and Canada. With the diversity of the people, the landscape of each place seen, and issues we all seem to deal with daily, there seems to be an endless supply of material for literature.

Section Title (Politics)

How Did Things get so off Course!

The agendas I see are not for you or for me. It seems so insane; they are for someone else's personal gain. They are not interested in yours or my voice; it is a matter of a single person's choice.

Is it the revenue that they seek, at the expense of those they consider to be weak? Maybe it is a need to feel control, to harness every sole. Or is it just some form of power sought to be gained, that cannot possibly be explained. Although some will try, it appears that logic passes them by.

What happened to all our rights, and putting up the good fight? As time passes by, I cannot help but wonder why. Most of us would just like some peace without being fleeced. So many folks that have gotten off course, with absolutely no remorse!

So, they tell me I have the right to vote

Even though we may have the right to vote, at times it makes no difference, as you may note. The laws we put in place, now become easy to erase.
I fear for our Children's future!

With all the political fights, it seems our fate is to lose all our rights. With the politicians fighting each other, not even trying to get along, even when they know their agendas are wrong. There are special interest groups with so much hatred and greed, they seem willing to do anything to succeed.

We are even having issues with our own Supreme court. Some of them have been appointed by one, and do not seem to be getting the right things done. Those who should be doing the best they can, appear to be following the agenda of just one man.

I know that some politicians' causes have merit and seem just, but then there is another side that I really don't trust. When there are two sides creating the country to split, maybe it is time to speak up and tell them to "Stop all this shit"?

Strong Women in the Whitehouse

When it comes to running this country, men have had their chance. With today's strong women, maybe it is our turn to step up and show them how to dance. At this time filled with hatred, bullying, and greed; it will take most women's votes in order to succeed.

As women, we have been pushed into the background for so many years, desperately trying not to show our disappointment with a river of tears. We need to stop the hatred, violence, and the desire to fight. Living peacefully on Earth should be everyone's birthright.

I do not want my children living through a civil war, as if we are playing some gruesome game where people keep score! It is my desire for everyone to see, this is not how life is supposed to be!

It is time for every woman to use her voice, to tell everyone else of an alternate choice. It is time to show everyone what woman can do, for the sake of the planet, for me and for you!

Juanita Kuwik

Hear my voice, it is still my choice!

If a woman wins the Presidential seat, what kind of challenges will she meet?
There are people who will try to manipulate the race, desperately trying to put a man in her place. Even with the opposition she will face, I am still hopeful that she will win this race.

Will she be the best choice made? I am both excited and afraid! How much intimidation can she take, and what kind of changes will she make?

Here is a thought for you to ponder, it is a thought that makes me wonder. At this time, should a woman choose to be a little naughty, there will be someone who thinks it is their right to tell her what to do with her body. By this thinking I should be able to say, every male should have a vasectomy by his eighteenth birthday. Now maybe you too can see, just how ridiculous this sounds to me!

It is my choice, so hear my voice! I choose not to go along with decisions that I know are wrong. We need a fresh choice, someone who will listen to our voice. Now I am sure that any person can tell me what I want to hear, but maybe it's her turn to shine this year.

Section Title (Life)

This is how I sea it!

As the beauty of the sun rises and sets, when I contemplate my accomplishments and regrets. There is just something about the sea, that both scares and comforts me. Both the smell of the kelp and the fish are reminders of things that I miss. With the ride of each wave, the fun memories I've saved.

The strength of the wave that is caught is not something that you can be taught. Just as soon as you think you've taken control, is the time you find out you'll be taking the roll. As you're rolling around in the wave, you'll be hoping it won't be your grave. When I think of life in the water that wants to eat me, there is also the darkness that I do see.

Whether it's cold or hot sand, just depends on where you stand. So, take heed when I say, "See something good in each day".

Watching the Moon Rise and Set

While I watch the dolphin play, I look forward to each day. With the returning darkness of the night, they get further from my sight. During the rising of this night's moon, I see the tide is coming soon. As I sit here on the beach, I contemplate the water's reach.

There are people walking by; a tired child begins to cry. I can see the child weep, as she is longing for some sleep. I do not fret for this wee lass, because this night will also pass. She will be up again very soon, with the setting of the moon.

What the Hell!

For all those times I think, "What the Hell"? Are all the same things you may think just as well. Like when I'm already speeding on the thruway; feeling like I need to step on the gas, because the dipstick behind me is running up my ass!

Asking at the drive-thru for a plain hamburger and plain bun, the person at the window tells me to pull into parking space one. Me and my one item in the express lane at the store, a person up front with thirty items or more.

When you stop somewhere for an afterwork drink, a person at the bar spills booze all over you and doesn't even blink. See what I mean, these things seem so obscene!

Life seen from inside the glass

When I stare out the window at the cars on this street, I often wonder about the diversity of the people I might meet. With the variety of the people I see every day, each one doing something different and going their own way.

Some with a smile on their face; others often running, as if in a race. There are people that pass by with a perpetual scowl, making me acutely aware of why animals growl. As these people pass by with a frown, makes me curious to know why their lives are so down.

A lady across the street in her garden bed, pulling up all the flowers and plants that are dead. There is a friendly postal worker that comes by each day, it always seems he has something pleasant to say.

I see the kids that pass by on their way to school, each one trying so desperately to be cool. Being cautious about the way they may speak, so that in front of their friends they don't appear to be weak.

While my mind seems to ponder people's highs and their lows, I still can't help wondering where each one will go.

Time Passes Too Quickly

Time passes more quickly as we get older, people's attitudes change seeming more sinical and colder. While I sit here alone feeling naked and afraid, my mind ponders the decisions I've made.

Is it just me, or is life just a balancing act for the whole world to see? Just when you think life is too heavy or bare, you'll see something wonderful showing us that people do care.

I look at the problems I face every day, and I try to remember there is another way. You may see things one minute as being a bit bleak, so just turn the corner and you may find what you seek.

When I look at my children, I still see the light, even though the world around us just doesn't seem right. We can't look at life having no reason or rhyme, because life is too short, there just isn't enough time.

Just one of many workplaces

The difficulties of this place, and the challenges we face!
Sometimes it seems there is no end to each day's tasks; often, help is provided if we just ask.

On a daily basis, I see happy and angry faces. Attitudes galore and so much more! So many personalities to explore. There have been those days when I feel like I want to walk out the door, but then I stop and wonder if I could be doing just a little bit more.

The strong family environment of this place forms a special kind of bond and comradery that cannot be erased. When people in the workplace come together doing what they should, at the end of the day, we can all feel good.

As I keep this in mind, everything seems to work out fine. I truly must say, I am still looking forward to every Friday!

Happy To Be Alive

I love as a child how I felt so invincible. Then when I got older, I became a little more sensible. Even as my thoughts on the future seem so unsure, I will always have the desire to endure.

Being one of our planet's boldest animals, we try to stand tall. Even when compared to the universe, we are really quite small.

We as Earth's children seem to be noticeably young, even though we still have no Idea of when life had begun. Did our lives really start here on Earth, or is this planet just a place of our birth?

Time may show that it is just not enough for us to survive. We as a species need to thrive. Even with life's obstacles we must overcome, I am still incredibly happy that our lives have begun.

I want to believe that everyone is good, but not everyone does as they know they should!

At Some point in your life, you may choose to take a husband or a wife. Marriage has become a topic of debate, so maybe your choice is considered a mate. Or maybe you choose no one at all, this really is your call.

Is being a good parent really inherent? Since we perceive ourselves as being a caring species, caring is something you would think we can teach, but for so many people this concept is completely out of reach. Values are a way of thinking that is taught, not something that can be bought.

Some people act in ways that they should. Showing us kindness, compassion, and a will to be good. Isn't this something we should all strive for, and maybe even just a little bit more? As I reach the end of each day, I would like to believe that most of us feel the same way.

But we all know of others consumed by so much hate, violence, and crime, which seems to me a complete waste of time. It should be a fact that we all know how to act!

Here is a thought you may have forgotten, for those of you who still choose to be rotten. Since time had begun, other animal rejects, are eaten or killed while they are still very young!

Excuses Made and Consequences Felt

Already a troubled child, at the age of six. Imagine the problems at sixteen, that cannot be fixed. As I tell you my thoughts, I know I am not alone; when I say to you, some discipline needs to be shown.

Is being a good neighbor, why I am expected to tolerate a child's poor behavior? Even after pondering this question a lot, the answer should still be, "I think not."

Have you ever noticed that with some people, the answers are consistently the same? There is always someone else to blame. When there is no abuse, it is just an excuse. The poor behavior that is allowed will affect us all somehow.

If as a parent this poem makes you mad, then I must say as the writer, this makes me glad. Stop making excuses when your child is bad!

Section Title (Love)

Love Lost & Found

I once fell in love with a man like no other. For the love that was lost, I will never recover. Do not get me wrong, it wasn't his choice. But I'm missing him now, his smile and his voice. Sometimes I feel I didn't do enough for his love. Now he looks down at me from above.

A love so enchanted that was taken for granted. The price that you pay will haunt you some day. The best we can do is hope dreams do come true. When time is at an end, we meet up once again.

But I keep this in mind at the end of each day, our children remind us of love here to stay. As I look at my children the one thing I see, is the man that I loved looking back at me. Each generation like the one before, reminds me of him and just a little bit more.

You don't need to say so!

I know that you love me! It is not for the things that I want you to say. Or the way that you look at the end of each day.

It is not for anything that you do, or the fact that you say you love me too. I knew from the start because it's felt in my heart.

Even when we do not always seem to be close, I still feel you love me the most. I know all of this because of each kiss, and when we are apart the love that I miss. I know that all of this is true, because of how much I really love you.

Watching the light fade

This is a poem about a woman who is charming, funny, with a heart of gold. While at the same time, she is strong and quite bold. As much as I love her so, sometimes I feel like I'm watching her go. I feel the need to hold her tight, so she doesn't slip away during the night.

I am certain the dementia she faces takes her to uncertain and scary places. This is a part of life I know I cannot erase, as I see the sadness and fear on her face.

I do feel some comfort in knowing; she has a special daughter & son, who seem to be trying hard to get the right things done. Even though I know this is true, it is breaking my heart, feeling that there is not enough I can do.

I miss you all!

There are times I just do not know what to say, when a loved one passes away. When I know the individual is in agonizing pain, it is enough to drive me insane. There is apparently no grief buffer, but I know for a fact that I do not want them to suffer.

Here is an interesting fact, overwhelming emotions are not something I lack. All I know is that I want my loved ones back!

Unfortunately, there are those who are only interested in what the missing person can give, it makes me wonder how these people can live. For some it may sound funny, but I cannot relate to people who are only interested in money.

Section Title (Family)

Yes, she is Daddy's Little Girl!

From the very start, you will love her with all your heart. With the softness of her touch to your very first finger clutch. While you tickle her toes, you will want to pinch her little nose.

With the passing of each day, she will change in so many ways. As each year will come and pass, you'll think she is growing up too fast.

When she gets older, you will see her getting bolder. Keep in mind that with the things you say and do, she will both love and hate you.

There will be times you will have to stand your ground; even when she says, she wishes you were not around! She will say things that are not always true, even when she really does love you.

She will always be your little girl, even with those times she makes your head swirl. Eventually you will see, the woman she turns out to be. If you are lucky enough by chance, you may even get to have a father daughter dance!

Sometimes A Little Diversity
Is Just What We Need

A little diversity is just what you'll see, when you encounter the men in our family tree. Intelligence and intellect are a couple of things that we get, along with some harshness we won't soon forget.

Even with the things they may say that can cut like a knife, I would not change a thing because of their importance in my life. As we all should, we take the bad with the good.

In other times when we are sad, hurt, or afraid, these are the times their strengths are displayed. When I am sometimes perplexed by the moods I might find, I still see the goodness and how they are kind. As you too may recall, these traits are a part of us all.

Our Cherry Blossom Tree

The strength of our family tree, and how each branch impresses me. Each of the women in my family tree, are all very different, but special to me.

As each one grows closer to me, I get to see their individuality.

Each with strengths all their own, make up stronger branches, so I'm never alone.

When the wind blows through each branch, you can see each one's beauty when given the chance. As our tree grows with each new blossom, our tree looks even more awesome! With the best of each woman there is no doubt, that's what this poem is all about.

The Puzzle Master

This is for my Fuzzy-Wuzzle; who takes each challenge in life, like a piece of a puzzle.
While he blows through each step with ease, I'm both befuddled and pleased. As I watch in confusion, he has already reached his conclusion.

He works and he plays on computers each day. Solving each problem, like there's nothing to stop him. With the complexity of each text, reminding me day after day, of how I am vexed.

I see the challenges that he will face and contemplate each decision he makes. As he goes through life like a quest, I wish nothing for him but the best.

She Taught Me Alot

What can I say about my mother? She grew up in life like so many others. I like to think she took care of me the best she could, even with the times that were not so good. Growing up herself in a harsher time, when sometimes people were not so kind.

Though she lived her life like a wounded dove, there were still those times that she did show love. With the way she lived in life that I could see, helps me to determine the person that I would like to be.

My not so distant, distant family!

One of the best things I can think about my mother, is the creation of my little brother. It is kind of ironic that even though we are miles apart, I still feel as if he is close to me, in my heart.

What can I say about his spouse, a man I have rarely seen outside the house. My brother's spouse from what I see, is an exceptionally good man who loves his family.

In the family of kids, there are six. I have to say an interesting mix. Three girls and three boys, all are too old for children's toys. Of each child I have to say, they are each one special in their own way.

These are people I like to see; because when I visited, they were all kind to me. It made me feel like such a winner, when one special lady cooked me dinner. Great Food! I miss them all!

One Special Poem for One Special Lady

Some days I am not certain what I should do, but today I am happy to be writing this poem just for you. Even seeing you just once in a while, you always manage to brighten my day with a smile.

When we were young you always knew what to do; in good times, bad times, and times we were blue. All the fond memories of you from when I was young. The crazy dances and songs that were sung. The family gatherings that you put together, no matter how good or how bad the weather.

I will always remember the first time I met you, and the rest of our motley crew. It was the day after a night; the entire family got into a fist fight. A birthday party at a place where one person decided someone else needed cake in their face. As the night turned into day, each person's boo-boos were on full display. I must say that it still puts a smile on my face when I think back to this crazy time and place! These are the memories I would never erase.

A large family is what you've got, and we all really love you a lot! I am sure I speak for most of us when I say, "I've come to love you more with each passing day.

Printed in the United States
by Baker & Taylor Publisher Services